The Making and Symbolism of
PAHARPUR *STUPA*
One of the oldest Buddhist tantric *stupas* in the world

Faruque Hasan

ISBN: 978-1-4457-0518-7

First published 2010

Copyright © Faruque Hasan, 2010

All rights reserved. No part of this publication may be reproduced, stored in a retrieval system or transmitted in nay form by any means, electronic, mechanical, photocopying, recording or otherwise, except brief extracts for the purpose of review, without the written permission of the copyright owner.

Price: USD 12.60

This book is dedicated to Dhiman and Vitapala, the father and the son, the sculptors of the 9th century AD Bangladesh, who were the initiators of the Bengal School of Sculpture.

Preface

Let us have a quick view of the history of Buddhism to understand the Paharpur *stupa* — the tantric *stupa* of the Great Monastery of Paharpur, and its background.

Gautama Buddha, the founder of Buddhism, was born in Lumbini in c. 623 BC, and raised in the small kingdom of Kapilavastu, both of which are in modern day Nepal. After the birth of his son, he renounced the temporal world to lead a life of an ascetic.

When Gautama was 35 years of age, he sat in a deep meditation under the Bodhi tree in Bodh Gaya, now a small town in Bihar — now a state of India. After 49 days in deep meditation, he attained enlightenment, thus became the Buddha or "The Enlightened One." From Bodh Gaya, Gautama Buddha went to Deer Park near Vārāṇasī (Benares) in northern India; and delivered his first sermon to the group of five companions.

For the remaining 45 years of his life, he traveled through northern India to preach his doctrine. According to a legend, to preach he came to Pundravardhana, one of the largest cities of that time in the subcontinent, which is now known as Mahasthangarh, and located in north Bangladesh.

The Buddha founded *Sangha* or the community of Buddhist monks and nuns to continue the dispensation of his doctrine. After his death, the *Sangha* held a number of Buddhist councils in order to reach consensus on matters of Buddhist doctrine and practices.

Three months after the Buddha had died the First Buddhist Council was convened in c. 498/9 BC, at Rajgir. This council compiled the *Vinayapitaka* — the code of ethics to be obeyed by the *Sangha*, monks and nuns.

The Second Buddhist council was held at Vaishali in 383 BC. The first schism in Buddhism occurred during this council, dividing the followers of Buddhism into two groups — *Sthaviras* and *Mahasanghikas*. The *Sthaviravāda* were the proponents of an orthodox understanding of the Buddha's teachings. Those who followed the old *Vinaya* - the regulatory framework for the Buddhist monastic community - edition were called the *Sthaviras*; and those who followed the new edition were called the *Mahāsāmghikas*.

During the reign of Emperor Ashoka (273-232 BC), Buddhism spread throughout northern India as the result of the personal initiative of the Emperor. Soon Buddhism crossed the border of India into other countries of Asia. It was first introduced in China during the Han dynasty – the second imperial dynasty of China (206 BC – 220 AD). The Chinese form of *Mahayana* later spread to Korea, Japan and Vietnam.

On the eve of the 1st century BC, the Buddhists of India faced the first religious persecution in the hands of King Pusyamitra (R. 185-151 BC), the founder and the first King of the Sunga Dynasty in Northern India. Pusyamitra Sunga was the commander-in-chief of the last Maurya emperor, a Buddhist ruler. He killed his mentor, and became the king. He persecuted Buddhists and helped the resurgence of Brahmanism. A Buddhist tradition holds him as "the number one enemy of the sons of the Sakyas (Buddhists), and a most cruel persecutor of the religion". The *Divyavadana (Divine Stories* — an anthology of Buddhist tales) ascribes to him the razing of *Stupas* and *Viharas* built by Ashoka, the placing of a bounty of 100 *Dinaras* (official currency of that time) upon the heads of Buddhist monks.

The *Fourth Buddhist Council* was held around 100 AD in Kashmir during the reign of Emperor Kanishka. The final schism in Buddhism into the *Mahayana* (literally meaning the 'great vehicle') and the *Hinayana* (literally meaning the 'lesser vehicle') or *Thervada* — 'doctrine of elders' took place during this council.

The followers of *Mahayana* believe that Buddha taught universal salvation. On the other hand, the aim of the followers of *Hinayana* is to attain the personal *nirvana*.

Tantric or esoteric tradition emerged in Indian Buddhism in the 4th century AD, and later became widespread in Tibet, and Japan. Its initiation ceremonies involve entry into a *mandala*, a mystic circle or symbolic map of the spiritual universe.

By the time of 5th century, Buddhism was already in decline in northern India, though at that time it was achieving multiple successes in Central Asia.

The period between the years 400 AD and 1000 AD saw gains by Vedic religion or Brahmanism, which after the 9th century became known as Hinduism, at the expense of Buddhism.

I-ching (634-c.712 AD), and Hsüan-tsang (602-664 AD) spoke of a decline of the Buddhist *Sangha* in India in the wake of the White Hun invasion in late 5th century AD.

The Chinese monk traveler, Hsüan-tsang, spent 17 years in India. He found a striking decline and relatively few followers of Buddhism in different parts of

India, with Hinduism and Jainism predominating. He also found relatively few Buddhists in Bengal, and Kamarupa (Assam). The land of Bengal comprises Bangladesh and Indian state of West Bengal. He wrote that Shashanka destroyed the Bodhi tree at Bodh Gaya and replaced Buddha statues with Shiva Lingams. Shashanka was the king of Gauda (Bengal) from 606 to 636 AD.

Buddhism revived again in Bengal and Bihar, and in no other part of the Indian subcontinent, under about 400 years long rule of Buddhist Pāla Dynasty. The first Pāla ruler, Gopala, whose fatherland was north Bangladesh, made Pundranagara (Mahasthangarh) his capital.

A *tantric* sect, an offshoot of *Mahayana,* evolved and thrived in Bengal and Bihar from the 8th century to the 12th century AD under the Pāla rule. It was the *tantric* sect of *Vajrayana* which gained ground in this region. This sect believed in the female divinities called *Taras*, who are the spouses of the Buddhas and Bodhisattvas. With the gradual decline of the Pāla rule in Bengal in the wake of the 12th century, *Vajrayana* disappeared gradually.

During the reign of Pāla rulers, five Buddhist learning seats became very prominent in their empire as well as in the outside world. They are: Nalanda, Vikramashila, Odantapuri, Somapura, and Jagaddala. These were actually Buddhist monasteries. Among these five monasteries, last four were built by the Pāla rulers, who were the followers of *Vajrayana* Buddhism. Somapura and Jagaddala are now located in Bangladesh; and Somapura is, at present, widely known as the 'Paharpur *Mahavihara*' or the Great Monastery of Paharpur. Paharpur *Stupa* stands in the center of the inner courtyard of the Paharpur *Mahavihara*.

Faruque Hasan
fqhasan@gmail.com

The making and symbolism of Paharpur *Stupa*

The ancient Sompura *Mahavihara*, the great monastery of Sompura, built by Emperor Dharmapala in between the years of circa 770-810 AD, is now known as the Paharpur *Mahavihara*. Dharmapala was the second ruler of the Pāla Dynasty, who ruled over Bangladesh along with a great part of north India.

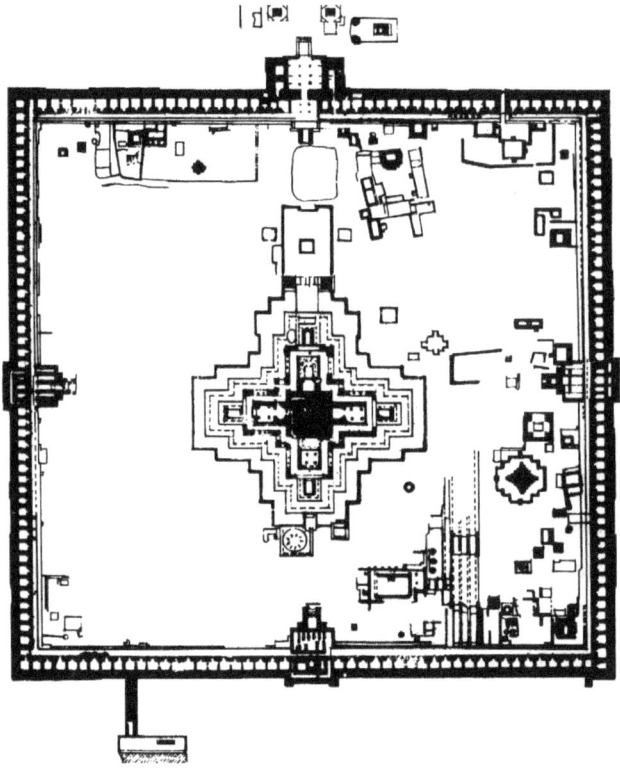

Plate - 1 Paharpur *Mahavihara* ground plan

The *mahavihara* is located in north Bangladesh. This part of the country is also known as Varendra/Varendri, and also was known as Pundra and Pundravrdhana during the ancient and medieval times. Varendri is the fatherland of the Pāla rulers (Rāmāchatitām, Shayandhakarnandi, 12 century AD). The Buddhist Pāla Dynasty ruled Bangladesh for about 350 years; from 750-1095 AD. Along with Bangladesh, they also ruled Magadha (Bihar), Assam, Orissa, and a part of Madhya Pradesh. All these lands are now in India. Pāla rule prolonged about fifty more years in Bihar after the dynasty had lost its foothold on its land of origin — the north Bangladesh.

According to Tibetan sources, during the Pāla Period, five great *mahaviharas* (monasteries) – Somapura (Paharpur), Jaggadala, Nalanda, Vikramshila and Odantapuri - formed a network under the state supervision. Among these five monasteries Paharpur *Mahavihara* and Jaggadala *Mahavihara* are in Varendri (north Bangladesh) and, located only a few kilometers apart.

In terms of acreage, Paharpur is the largest of the *mahaviharas* in the world. The quadrangle monastery is 281.025 meters in length from north to south and 280.111 meters, from east to west.

Plate – 2 Paharpur *Stupa*

The colossal *stupa*[1] of the Paharpur *Mahavihara* stands approximately in the center of the inner courtyard of it. The *mahavihara* belonged to the *Vajrayana* sect of Buddhism, the predominant sect of that time, in Varendra (north Bangladesh), Vanga (east Bangladesh), Samatata (south and southeast Bangladesh), Radha (south West Bengal), and Magadha (south Bihar). Except a part of Samatata, all these lands were the parts of the great Pāla Empire.

Vajrayana is one of the tantric sects of Buddhism; and Bengal, comprising Bangladesh and West Bengal state of India, is considered as the birth place of *tantra*.[2]

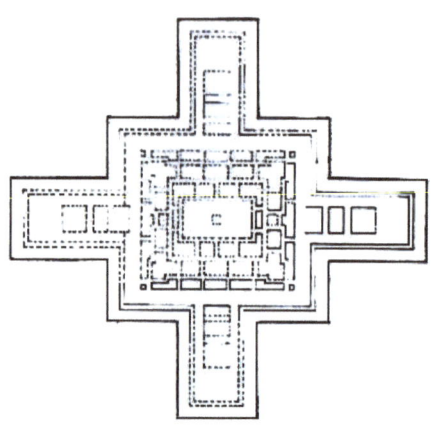

Plate - 3 Bharat Bhayna *Stupa* ground plan

The Paharpur *Stupa*, made of baked bricks laid in mud mortar, is a cruciform, pyramidal *stupa* rising from the ground plan in three gradually diminishing tiers. The cruciform *stupa* first appeared in Bangladesh. The Bharat Bhayna *Stupa*, also made of baked bricks, in the southwest part of Bangladesh is the oldest cruciform *stupa* in the world discovered till now. Southwest, south, east beyond Megna River and southeast parts of Bangladesh, were known, at that time, as *Samatata* means a land at sea level.

Plate - 4 Bharat Bhayna *Stupa*

The octagonal Bharat Bhayna *Stupa* was built in the middle of the fifth century AD. The east-west arm of the *stupa* is 99.4 meters long; and north-south arm, 95.4 meters long. No trace of any monastery attached to this *stupa* has been found. Perhaps, the monastery, which the *stupa* belonged to, was made of wood or other perishable building materials. At that time, the Buddhist monasteries used to be built mostly with perishable building materials. The Bharat Bhayna was one of the 30 great *Sangaramas*[3] in Samatata mentioned by Hsüan-tsang, the famous Chinese Monk-traveler, who visited Bangladesh including Samatata during the years in between 637 to 645 AD.

The Bharat Bhayna *Stupa* was not only a *stupa;* it was a *stupa*-cum-temple as well. This was another remarkable feature of the unique ancient Buddhist architecture in Bangladesh that in this land the *stupa* transformed into *stupa-cum-temple*. The second oldest cruciform *stupa*-temple in Bangladesh, as well as in the world, is the Salban *Vihara stupa*, built in the middle of the seventh century AD at Mainamati in Samatata, now in the southeast part of Bangladesh.

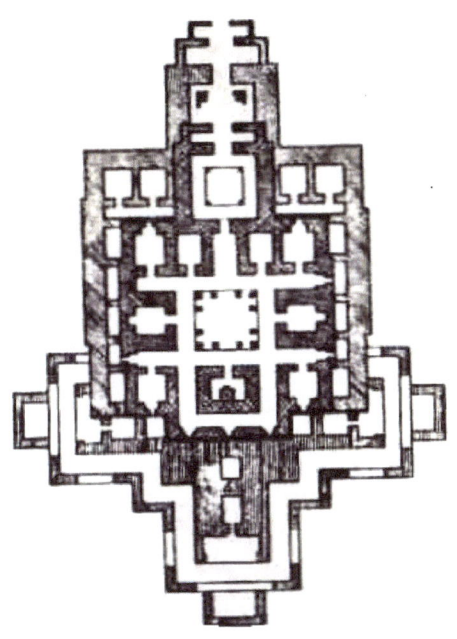

Plate - 5 Salban *Vihara Stupa* ground plan

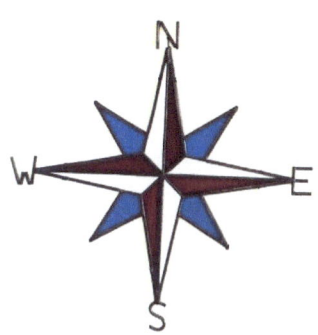

8-point compass rose

In the center of the Salban *Vihara*'s inner courtyard, on the virgin soil, about 6.6 meters under the present ground level, the ruins of a cruciform *stupa*, belonged to the monastery's first and second occupation periods, has been discovered (Nazimuddin, 1966). The first occupation period of the Salban *Vihara* covers the years from 650 to 750 AD; and the second occupation period, from 750 to 800 AD. Each arm of the Salban *stupa*, which belongs to its third occupation period, and built on the *stupa* of the previous two periods, measures about 51.8 meters. The Bharat Bhayna *Stupa* symbolizes, among other things, an 8-point compass rose; but Salban *Stupa* is a 16-point compass rose showing 16 directions.

A compass rose is a figure which displays the orientation of the cardinal directions — north, south, east, and west, as well as the intermediate directions. In the Middle Ages map makers moved to the 16-point rose. The earliest 32-point compass rose was developed by Arab navigators also during the Middle Ages.

The square Salban *Vihara* is a little bit more

than half of the size of the Paharpur *Mahavihara*, and measures 167.64 meters on all sides.

During the forth occupation period (ninth century AD), the north part of the *stupa* was change into an oblong shape; which deformed its original cruciform shape. In the next occupation period (the fifth period: 900-1050 AD), the oblong plan of its north part was retained. The remains of the Period VI are too scanty to give any idea of the shape and plan of the structure. The Salban *Vihara* was abandoned, perhaps, in later 14th century.

The monastery and other Buddhist structures in Mainamoti were almost destroyed during the end part of the Second World War by the military contractors to collect bricks from them to build a cantonment and an airfield for the British Army, while the Japanese Army was knocking at the border of India from Myanmar.

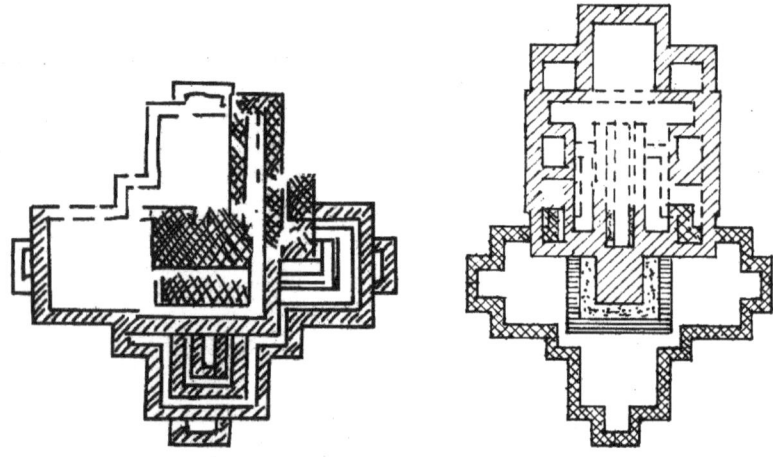

Plate - 6 Ranir Banglow *Stupa*   Plate - 7 Ananda *Vihara Stupa*

At least four more cruciform *stupa*-temples were built in between eighth to twelfth centuries at Mainamoti. They are: Ananda *Vihara Stupa* (c.8th/9th century), Voj *Vihara Stupa* (c.8th-12th centuries), Rupban Mura *Stupa* (7th century) and Ranir Banglow *Stupa* (c.12th -13th centuries). The cruciform *stupas* of Ananda *Vihara*, and Ranir Banglow have also been partially deformed in shape during later periods.

During the Pāla Period, which stretched about 350 years – from 750 to 1095 AD in Bangladesh, southeast part of the country, at that time known as

Samatata, was not under the Pāla rule; rather ruled by different small dynasties, most of them were Buddhist. But southwest part of Samatata, where the Bharat Bhayna *Stupa* is located, became a part of Pāla Empire during the rule of Emperor Dharmapala.

As mentioned earlier, Bharat Bhayna is a cruciform *stupa* (as well as a temple). The cross is one of the most ancient human symbols, and is used by many religions. The cross represents the union of the concepts of divinity, the vertical line; and the world, the horizontal line (Koch, 1955). At the same time, it is a representation of the division of the world into four elements (Chevalier, 1997) – earth, water, air and fire; and of four cardinal points or directions– east, west, north and south.

Bharat Bhayna *Stupa* has an angle of projection in between each two arms of its cross (Plate – 3). Its four angles of projection between the arms are pointing to four additional directions – *Īśānya* (northeast), *Āgneya* (southeast), *Vāyavya* (northwest), *Nairṛti* (southwest). The Bharat Bhayna with its eight projections, like a *Dharma Chakra*, represents the Noble Eightfold Path[4] factors of Buddhism – Right view, Right intention, Right speech, Right action, Right livelihood, Right effort, Right mindfulness, and Right concentration.

Plate 8 *Dharma Chakra*

In Buddhism, the four Great Elements, *Mahābhūta,* are earth, water, fire and air. *Mahābhūta* is generally synonymous with *catudhātu*, which is Pāli for the "Four Elements." The Four Elements are a basis for the understanding of and the liberating oneself from suffering. Four arms of the Bharat Bhayna cross represent the *catudhātu*.

Vayu/Pavan (Air/Wind)

Ap/Jala (Water)   *Akasha* (Aether/Space)   *Agni/Teja* (Fire)

Prithvi/Bhumi (Earth)

Plate - 9 *Mahābhūta*

Cross of a Buddhist *stupa* also represents Four Noble Truths or The Four Truths of the Noble Ones (Sanskrit: *catvāri āryasatyāni*; Pali: *cattāri ariyasaccāni*), which is one of the most fundamental Buddhist teachings. In broad terms, these truths relate to suffering or *dukkha,* (1) its nature, (2) its origin, (3) its cessation and (4) the path leading to its cessation. Each arm of a cruciform *stupa* represents one of these four truths.

The ground plan of a *Mahayana stupa, e.g.* Rupban Mura *Stupa*, the Inca Cross – *Chakana,* the Greek cross, a *Mandala*[5], a *Yantra*[6,] and the ground plan of the Bharat Bhayna *Stupa* are amazingly similar (Plates 11, 12, 13, 14, 15, 16). In Greek cross as well as in Bharat Bhayna *Stupa* the arms have been elongated, and they both are of equal-armed cross.

Plate - 10 Rupban Mura *Stupa*

Rupban Mura *Stupa* and its attached monastery, built in the 9th/10th century AD, are located, along with at least fifty more ruins of Buddhist monasteries and *stupas* belonged to 6th to 13th centuries, at Mainamoti — once the capital of a small Buddhist kingdom, Samatata, in the east part of Bangladesh.

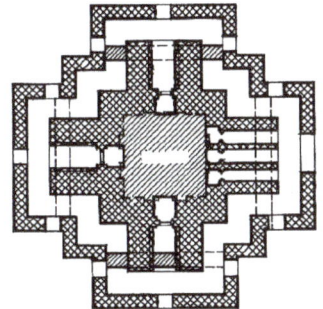
Plate – 11 Rupban Mura *Stupa*

Plate - 12 Inca Cross

Plate - 13 Greek cross

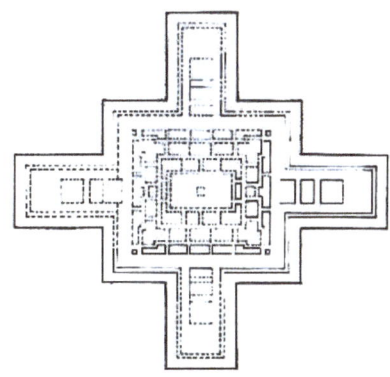
Plate - 14 Bharat Bhayna

Plate - 15 *Mandala*

Plate - 16 *Yantra*

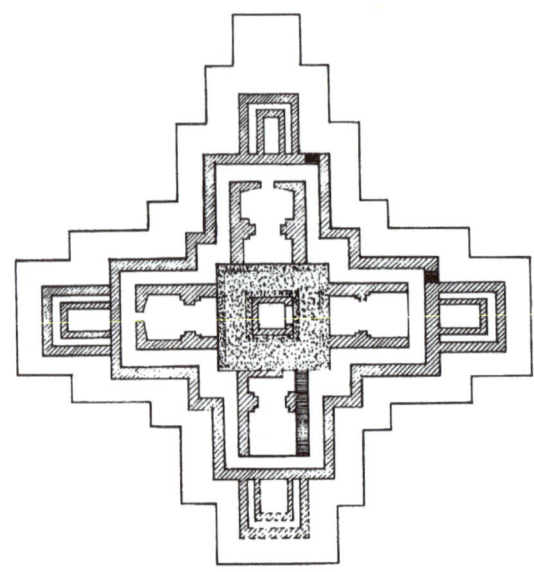

Plate - 17 Paharpur *Stupa* ground plan

It is most likely that the conceptual and structural idea of the Paharpur *Stupa* developed from that of the Salban *Stupa*, which in its turn developed from that of the Bharat Bhayna *Stupa*. As like as in Salban *Vihara Stupa*, the Paharpur *Stupa* has three angles of projection in between each of the two arms, instead of one as in the Bharat Bhayna *Stupa*.

In the Paharpur *Stupa*, a 16-point compass rose, symbolism is much more intricate then that in the *stupas* similar to it. In Bharat Bhayna, the *stupa* was in two tiers – a raised base/platform and a shrine built on the platform. The Paharpur *Stupa* is a three-tier structure rises from the ground plan in gradually diminishing tiers. The gradually diminishing tiers give it a look of a stepped pyramid. The third tier of the *stupa* is a temple. The outline of the cruciform temple, the third tier, with one angle of projection in between each two arms of the cross corresponds exactly to that of the Bharat Bhayna's ground plan.

Plate – 18 The Paharpur *Stupa*

The imposing Paharpur *Stupa* is 108.66 meters in length from north to south; and 95.78 meters, from east to west. It covers about 10407 sq. meters of area. In its present ruinous condition, being devoid of its pinnacle – the *chhatri/sikhara*, it still stands 21.95 meters tall on the ground.

The three tiers of the Paharpur *Stupa* represent three jewels of Buddhism – Buddha, the preacher – Gautama Buddha; *dhamma*, the doctrine; and the *sanga*, the community formed by Gautama Buddha with his ten disciples. From the base of the *stupa*, the first tier is the Buddha; the second tier, *dhamma*; and the third tier, the *sanga*. The three tiers also represent the three levels of Buddhist cosmology, *Kāmadhātu* (the world of desire), *Rupadhātu* (the world of forms) and *Arupadhātu* (the world of formlessness). They may symbolize from above to down, the haven, the earth and the underworld – the World Tree.

Each of the upper two tiers of the *stupa* has, around it, a circumambulatory path, enclosed by parapet walls, for the use by the devotees. The circumambulatory walk of the lowest tier is open.

Plate - 19 Sanctum/*garbhagriha* of Paharpur *stupa*

The upper terrace of the Paharpur *Stupa* has four rectangular sanctums – *garbhagriha*, one in each cardinal direction, and each facing an assembly hall – *mandapa* – standing in the fore ground. The four sanctums are clustered around a centrally placed hollow pile that originates from the podium and ends at the surviving top level of the *stupa*. This hollow represents the void or the ether – the fifth Great Element.

The four sanctums of the Paharpur *Stupa* are standing on the four arms of its cross. In these four sanctums of the *stupa* were placed colossal statue of four spiritual/*dhyani* Buddhas[7] – statue of one spiritual Buddha in each sanctum in accordance to his attributes. Thus, the statue of Aksobhya in '*Bhumi Sparsha Mudra*' or touching earth gesture, who dwells to the east, was placed in the sanctum facing the east; the statue of Ratanasambhava in '*Varada Mudra*' or boon giving/giving oneself gesture, who dwells to south direction, was placed in the sanctum facing the south; the statue of Amoghasiddhi in '*Abhaya Mudra*' or fearlessness gesture, who dwells to the north direction, was placed in the sanctum facing the north; and the statue of Amitabha in '*Dhyana Mudra*' or meditation/'*Samadhi*' gesture, who dwells to the west direction, was placed in the sanctum facing the west.

Plate - 20 The bronze statue of Paharpur *Mahavihara*

During the excavation at the Paharpur monastery premises in 1982, at the monastic cell number 37, a highly damaged bronze made Buddha statue has been discovered. The statue has been damage by fire, perhaps, during the Kamboja[9] invasion of the monastery in circa 1000 AD. The Kambojas set fire to the monastery. The incident may also took place during ransack of the monastery by *Vangala*[10] army let by Jatavarman, a Hindu king of Vanga-Samatata, in the last quarter of the eleventh century AD. The torso of the statue is 1.27 meters long; its lower part is missing. Jatavarman put fire to the monastery. It is thought that the statue was place in one of the sanctums of the *stupa*-temple (Nazimuddin, 1997).

The colossal statues of the spiritual Buddhas of Paharpur *Stupa* were made, perhaps, of stucco as like as those of the spiritual Buddhas of Vikramshila *Stupa* made of. None of the stucco statues, buried under the debris for a long time, could survive the onslaught of time, and torrential rains of Bangladesh. Or, during the rule of Sena Dynasty (c.1095-1204 AD), which replaced the Pāla Dynasty in Bangladesh, the statues were destroyed by the Sena kings, who were Hindu by faith; the first two of them, who were *Saivite*[8] and ruled from c.1095-1178 AD, were extremely intolerant to Buddhism. During their rules, the followers of Buddhism in Bangladesh started worshiping Hindu gods and goddesses to save themselves from the wrath of the ruler; though in secret they remained Buddhists.

It may be mentioned here that both the Paharpur *Mahavihara* and the Vikramshila *Mahavihara* were built by Emperor Dharmapala (c.770-810AD). Perhaps, Paharpur *Mahavihara* was built after the Vikramshila *Mahavihara* had been built. This postulation may be drawn from the fact that the Vikramshila *Mahavihara* has a two-tier *stupa*, where as the Paharpur *Mahavihara* has a three-tier *stupa*; that means the *stupa* of Paharpur is more advance in architectural design and symbolism than that of Vikramshila.

The three angles of projection in between each two arms of the Paharpur *Stupa* cross have made it a thirty six sided structure. In traditional Buddhist thought, people are said to have 36 passions. Each side of the Paharpur *stupa* stands, probably, for one of these 36 passions.

According to Buddhism, 36 passions arise from 18 feelings. Each of these feelings can be either attached to pleasure or detached from pleasure. People perceive these feelings through their six senses – sight, sound, smell, taste, touch and consciousness. Each of the 36 passions may be manifested in the past, present or future; and thus makes 108 *klesas* or afflictions that people may have.

The ground plan of the Paharpur *Stupa* is a specific *yantra/mandala*[5] or a geometric diagram used in tantric practices. From the top view, the *stupa* architecture appears to be a three dimensional *'yantra/mandala'*. 'The *mandalic* structure may be indicated by geometrical lines, by figurative representations or, mostly, a combination of both. ....A concentric cross or star plan is no less than a *manadala* then a square or a circle" (Gail, 1999).

On the lower part of the basement walls of the Paharpur *Stupa*, now covered under about 1.25 meters thick depository soil, there are sixty three stone sculptures of deities. Except one of these sculptures, the one of Padmapani, all others are of Hindu gods and goddesses. In the Indian subcontinent, Buddhism treats Hindu gods and goddesses as the deities of lower stratum. So, by putting them on the basement walls, perhaps, they have been assigned with the job of security guards of the *stupa* as well as of its *mandala*.

Plate – 21 Stone statues on the basement walls

Most of the sculptures on the plinth walls of the *stupa* have, approximately, the same height as of the plinth, and are made of the same kind of material – sand stone.

The lower part of the basement of Paharpur *Stupa*, containing the stone sculptures, has not been exposed by archaeological excavation due to the water logging problem arises inside the monastery during the months of monsoon. The ground level outside the monastery is now higher than the ground level of its inner courtyard, which was, surely, not the case when the monastery was built more than twelve hundred years back. The difference between the ground levels, at present, is about 1.2 meters. The land of Bangladesh, which is an active delta, raises five millimeters, in average, a year due to gradual deposition of silt. Thus the ground level outside the monastery has gradually become higher than the ground level of the inner courtyard of it. This difference in ground levels creates a serious water logging problem in the inner courtyard during months of monsoon.

A river, known as Nur/Ennar River, which is now dead, used to flow a few meters off the monastery's south wall. The well developed drainage system of the monastery, including the *stupa*, was connected to this river. At present a river flows about fifteen kilometers away from the monastery. The present water logging problem of the monastery may be solved by connecting its drainage system to this river.

Plate - 22 Terracotta plaques on the *Stupa* wall

The walls of the second and third tiers of the Paharpur *stupa* possess two rows of terracotta plaques set in recessed panels; most of them are rectangular in size, depicting deities, mythical figures, scenes from folk and social lives etc. The upper part of the basement walls possesses only one row of terracotta plaques. About 2,800 terracotta plaques used to embellish the walls of the *stupa*. Many of them are still *in situ* on the walls. The terracotta plates are mostly in the size of 20.3 cm – 35.6 cm in broad side, and 21.6 cm in height. The parts of the walls, which are not covered with terracotta plaques, were, perhaps, covered with stucco plaster.

The Paharpur *Stupa* had only one entrance, through the flight of steps, from the north. It means that it had only one *torana*/gate instead of four in four cardinal directions, which is the norm in a *Mahayana stupa*.

To build the Bharat Bhayna *Stupa*, the cellular architecture was used. In this style of architecture, blind cells would be built, sometimes, in tiers, and then packed solidly with earth to raise a platform or a basement on which a superstructure used to be built. The same architecture was used to build Paharpur *Stupa*. The cellular architecture was a unique style of architecture evolved in Bangladesh.

The best example, in Bangladesh, of a raised platform to build a Buddhist *stupa*/temple is the Gokul Medh in Mahasthangarh or Pundranagar, built in 6th/7th century AD about 70 kilometers south of Paharpur. The *stupa*/temple on top of the platform is no more there. The platform is approximately 13 meters in height from the level of the surrounding plain.

S.K. Saraswati (1943) agreed with N.K. Dikshit's (1938) idea that a four-faced Jain temple, which probably existed earlier at the site, could have served as a model of the Paharpur *stupa*-temple plan. In fact, it is Bharat Bhayna *Stupa*-temple which served as a model of the Paharpur *stupa*-temple plan, not a Jain temple.

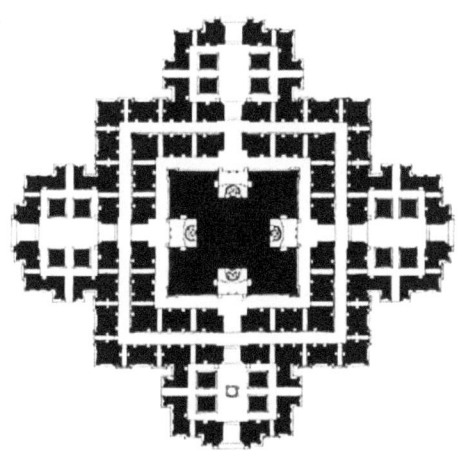

Plate - 23 Ananda Temple ground plan

The design of the Paharpur *Stupa* is quite unusual as it has "none of the characteristics features of Indian temple architecture......." The style of architecture of Bharat Bhayna, Salban, and Paharpur *stupa*-temples as well as monasteries has most profoundly influenced the Buddhist temple architectures of Myanmar, Indonesia (Java), and Cambodia. The Bharat Bhayna-Salban-Paharpur plans appear to have, substantially, influenced the *Candi* Kalasan of 778 AD, *Candi* Sevu of c. 9th century AD; both are at Prambanan in Java; and Ananda Temple of c. 1090 AD at Bagan/Pagan in Myanmar. Ananda Temple followed the ground plan of Bharat Bhayna (Plate - 3). The temple is a pyramidal pagoda like that of Paharpur, rather than the bell-shaped *stupa* that are common in Myanmar. The central structure of the Temple has remained relatively unchanged since it was built, but its long corridors from the outer wall to the central structure have been added in the 19th century.

Plate - 24 Candi Sevu ground plan

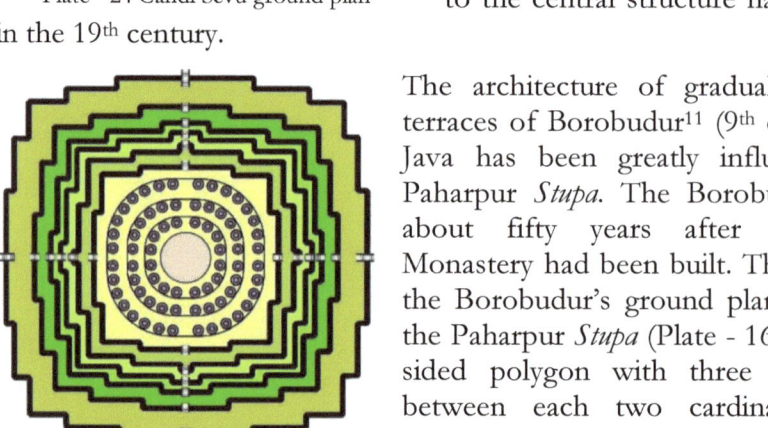

Plate - 25 Ground plan of Borobudur

The architecture of gradually diminishing terraces of Borobudur[11] (9th century AD) in Java has been greatly influenced by the Paharpur *Stupa*. The Borobudur was built about fifty years after the Paharpur Monastery had been built. The outer line of the Borobudur's ground plan, as like as of the Paharpur *Stupa* (Plate - 16), is a thirty six sided polygon with three projections in between each two cardinal arms; only difference is that in Borobudur the cardinal arms of the cross pointing to the four cardinal directions are not elongated as like as those arms in the Paharpur *Stupa*.

---

1. *Stupa*, literally meaning "heap", is a mound-like structure. The earliest Buddhists would not make any Buddha statues; instead they used to make *stupa*, made of mud or clay, as the symbol of Gautama Buddha's burial mound — an object of veneration. Gradually, it has become a symbol of enlightened/awakened mind as well as the

symbol of Buddhism. Some *Stupas* contain Buddhist relics — the remains of the Gautama Buddha or a Buddhist saint.

2. "The word *tantra* means 'to manifest, to expand, to show and to weave.' *Tantrism* is marked by a rejection of orthodox Vedic tenets. *Tantra* deals primarily with spiritual practices and ritual forms of worship, which aim at liberation from ignorance and rebirth. Rather than a single coherent system, *tantra* is an accumulation of practices and ideas which is characterized by the use of ritual, by the use of the mundane to access the supra-mundane, and by the identification of the microcosm with the macrocosm. Its purpose is to achieve complete control of oneself, and of all the forces of nature, in order to attain union with the cosmos and with the divine. *Vajrayana* is a *tantric* sect of Buddhism. There are other sects of *tantric* Buddhism. *Vajrayana* teaches that in order to access esoteric knowledge, the practitioner requires initiation from a skilled spiritual teacher or guru known as *shidha* guru.

Śāntarakṣita **(725–788)**, the abbot of Nalanda *Mahavihara* in early 8th century AD, founded the philosophical school known as the *Yogacara-Svatantrika-Madhyamaka*, which united the *Madhyamaka* tradition of Nagarjuna and the *Yogacara* tradition of Asanga with the logical and epistemological thought of *Dharmakirti*. Śāntarakṣita was the prince of a small kingdom, Samvar, which is now known as Savar and located about 17 km north of Dhaka City. Śāntarakṣita introduced *tantric* Lama Buddhism in Tibet. Padmasamvava, known as Guru Rimpoche in Tibet, and born in Sowat Valley now in Pakistan, was a disciple and the brother-in-law of Śāntarakṣita as he (Padmasamvava) married his sister. Śāntarakṣita recommended Padmasamvava to the king of Tibet when the king was seeking a guru to reform Buddhism in his kingdom.

Atisa Dipankara, who reformed Lamaism in Tibet in 10th century, was born in the village of Vajrajogini, located about 27 km south of Dhaka City.

3. *Sangharama* is a Sanskrit word meaning "temple" or "monastery", the place, including its garden or grove, where dwells the Buddhist monastic community or *Snagha*.

4. The Noble Eightfold Path describes the way to the end of suffering, as it was laid out by Siddhartha Gautama. It is a practical guideline to ethical and mental development with the goal of freeing the individual from attachments and delusions; and it finally leads to understanding the truth about all things. In the Noble Eightfold Path, great emphasis is put on the practical aspect, because it is only through practice that one can attain a higher level of existence and finally reach *Nirvana*.

5. "*Mandala* is a concentric diagram having spiritual and ritual significance in both Buddhism and Hinduism. In various spiritual traditions, *mandalas* may be employed for focusing attention of aspirants and adepts, as a spiritual teaching tool, for establishing a sacred space, and as an aid to meditation and trance induction. In common use, *mandala* has become a generic term for any plan, chart or geometric pattern that represents the cosmos metaphysically or symbolically, a microcosm of the Universe from the human perspective."

6. *Yantra* is a Sanskrit word for instrument or machine. The word derived from the root *yam* meaning to control or subdue or "to restrain, curb, check". In mysticism, it is a symbol of geometric figures used to balance the mind or focus it on spiritual concepts. A geometric symbol of *yantra* depicts both macrocosmic and microcosmic forces acting together - the movement towards and away from the centre - control and liberation within the one device. Mantra plus *yantra* creates *tantra*. "The term *yantra* normally refers to Hindu contexts and practices, while *mandala* normally refers to Buddhist contexts and practices. Yet, the terms are also used interchangeably, and *mandala* is sometimes used as a cross-over term in Hindu contexts."

7. In *Vajrayana* Buddhism, the Five *Dhyani* Buddhas are representations of the five qualities of the Buddha. *Dhyani* means who is in meditation.

8. *Shaivism* is the oldest sect of Hinduism. A follower of *Shaivism* is called *Shaiva*, or *Saivite*. The followers of this sect revere Shiva as the Supreme Being. According to Hinduism, he is the god of reproduction and the destruction – a quintessential destroyer he is. He forms the trio of supreme gods with Brahma and Vishnu.

9. The Kamboja was a tribe of Iron Age India possibly of Iranian/Scythian origin. Kamboja Kingdoms were located beyond Gandhara in the extreme north-west of the Indian subcontinent. The place is now located in Pakistan. Some scholars describe the ancient Kambojas as a section of the Indo-Aryans; few others style them as probably Indo-Iranian. During Indo-Scythian invasion of India before Kushan Period (130 BC – AD 185), Kambojas appear to have migrated to Gujarat, Southern India, Sri Lanka and later to Bengal (Bangladesh + West Bengal) and Cambodia.

10. During ancient time, middle part of Bangladesh was known as *Bôngo/Bangla/Vangala*. Later on, the whole geographical region comprising Bangladesh, the Indian state of West Bengal and some parts of the neighboring Indian states of Bihar, Assam, Tripura and Orissa became known as *Bôngo* as well as *Bangla*.

11. The guru of the Shylendra king, who built Borobudur, was a Bengali monk. The Buddhist Shylendra Dynasty of East Asia was of South Indian origin. The Shylendra kings had close relationship with the Buddhist Pāla rulers of Bengal and Magadha.

Appendix

PAHARPUR *MAHAVIHARA* — THE GREAT MONASTERY OF PAHARPUR

Bangladesh was the last Buddhist retreat in the South Asian subcontinent, also known as Indian subcontinent — the birthplace of Buddhism. In the past, the country had, across it, a great number of Buddhist monasteries and *stupas*. At present, the relics of only a few of these ancient monasteries and *stupas* can be traced out. The Paharpur *Mahavihara* or the Great Monastery of Paharpur is the most renowned one among these relics. This colossal *Mahavihara* has been included, in the year of 1985, in the list of World Cultural Heritage by the UNESCO.

The relic of the Paharpur *Mahavihara* is located at Paharpur — a village in Nawgaon district, about 285 kilometers off to the north-west of Dhaka, the capital city of Bangladesh.

The monastery was built by Emperor Dharmapala, who reigned over Bangladesh, along with some other parts of India, during the period of c.770-810 AD; hence the monastery was officially named as Dharmapala *Mahavihara* after the name of its builder. *Mahavihara* is a compound word; *maha* means huge, great, vast etc., and *vihara*, a learning center as well as an abode of Buddhist monks.

The *Mahavihara* was built on the bank of a river known as Nur or Ennar River. The river is no more there. Its bed has got dried up long ago.

Besides Paharpur *Mahavihara*, Emperor Dharmapala built some other great monasteries, such as Vikrampuri *Mahavihara*, Vikramsila *Mahavihara* and Odantapuri *Mahavihara* etc. He was the patron of Nalanda *Mahavihara*, now located in India, and at that time was within his empire. All these monasteries were very large and renowned as learning centers during ancient time.

The Paharpur *Mahavihara* was also known as the Shompuri *Mahavihara*, when the name of the village, where it is located, was Shompur. Before the archaeological excavation was done, the 21.95 meters high ruin of the central *stupa* of the *Mahavihara*, with the dense vegetation grown on it, used to look like a mound or hillock on a plain land; so the name of the village changed from Shompur into Paharpur and the great monastery has locally become known as Paharpur *Mahavihara*. The word, *Pahar* means hill; and the suffix '*pur*' denotes a city or a town.

In the earlier period, Buddhist monasteries in the South Asian subcontinent used to be built of wood and bamboos. In the beginning, monasteries were the recess during the rainy season for Buddhist monks. From simple dwelling houses built for monks, some of these monasteries gradually turned into learning centers for them; the bigger ones even turned into as like as the residential university in modern sense. Besides Buddhism, logic, grammar, philology, medical science, comparative religious studies, civil engineering, astronomy and some other secular subjects used to be taught at Paharpur *Mahavihara*; so, it can be said that, this monastery was one of the earliest 'universities' in Bangladesh as well as in the world.

The Paharpur *Mahavihara*, with a *stupa* in the center of its inner courtyard and a *Tara* temple, stands on eleven hectares of land. This huge building structure, sans the *Tara* Temple, was the result of a single period of construction. In Nalanda, eight monasteries, three temples, one *Chayta* and an administrative building cover fourteen hectares of land.

The Potala Palace Monastery in Tibet is a huge monastery; but it is not a single structure, and it is not purely a monastery. The Potala Palace Monastery consists of one red building known as the Red Palace, one white building known as the White Palace and a numerous ancillary buildings. Besides being a monastery, it was also the sit of the Tibetan government led by the Dalai Lama, and a home to a large printing press.

A lot of followers of Jainism were there in Bangladesh at the beginning of the Pāla rule, which began in 750 AD; though its influence had been declining fast vis-à-vis to the increasing influence of Buddhism on the people of the country. By the end of the eighth century, Jainism completely disappeared from Bangladesh to give way to Buddhism to become the predominant faith of the people at that time.

When the famous Chinese monk traveler, Hsüan-tsang, visited Bangladesh during the years of 637 to 645 AD, he found in the country the followers of the Brahmanism and the Jainism greater in numbers than the followers of the Buddhism.

In the 9th century AD, Brahmanism underwent a great reformation led by Shankaracharya; and the faith became known as Hinduism.

Emperor Dharmapala was the second in line of the Pāla rulers of Bangladesh. These rulers used to profess Buddhist faith. They belonged to the *Vajrayana* sect of Buddhism. Besides Bangladesh, a great part of Bihar and some parts of Oryssa and Assam were also within the boundary of the Pāla Empire.

The glory of the Paharpur *Mahavihara* started eclipsing after about two hundred and fifty years of its construction at the weakening of the Pāla Dynasty. In the beginning of the 11th century, Divya or Divyoka, a Hindu chieftain from the Eastern Bangladesh, rebelled against the 12th Pāla King, Mahipala - II. He killed the King, occupied Varendra or the north part of Bangladesh, and caused havoc to the Paharpur *Mahavihara*. Ramapala, the brother of the slain King, was able to regain Varendra from Vima, the successor of Divya. He rebuilt the burnt down monastery. He also built the Jagaddala *Vihara* a few kilometers off the Paharpur *Mahavihara*.

The Pāla Dynasty ruled Bangladesh from the year of 750 AD to till the year of 1095 AD. On the eave of 13th century, the most part of Bangladesh went under the sway of the Sena rule. Sena rulers were Hindu by faith; the first two of them were very much intolerant to Buddhism. During their rules, the gradual declination of Buddhism in Bangladesh as well as the Paharpur *Mahavihara* set their feet.

A lot of terracotta plaques of Hindu motifs on the walls of the Paharpur *Stupa* suggest that during this period, most of the terracotta plaques of Buddhist motifs were replaced with that of Hindu motifs; and the *Mahavihara* turned into a Hindu temple.

The Sena kings ruled all over Bangladesh till the year of 1204. In that year, Laksmansena, the third in succession of the Sena kings, lost his control over the north part of Bangladesh to the Khalji Turks led by Ikhtiaruddin Muhammad Bakhtiar Khalji. Khaljis came from the Central Asia. Ikhtiaruddin destroyed Nalanda *Mahavihara* being instigated by the Hindu Brahmin of that place, taking it mistakenly as a fort.

The Turks and the subsequent rulers of Bangladesh — Afghans, Arabs and Mughals — were Muslims by faith. During their rules a mass conversion of the people mostly from Buddhism to Islam has made this country predominantly Muslim. In the country, the preaching of Islam in large scale started in the beginning of 14th century, almost one hundred years after the Turks had conquered its north part. It was the Sufis who led the preaching, not being much encouraged by the rulers.

During the Turk to the Mughal periods, without the royal patronage and the support from the people, the maintenance of the Paharpur *Mahavihara*, a huge monastery, became very difficult. So, it fell to declination, was gradually abandoned by its inmates, and then with the passage of time got lost in oblivion.

While lying abandoned for centuries, jungle grew all over the monastery; and hidden from the sight of the human beings with the dense jungle, its lofty central *stupa* crumbled down by its own weight. The torrential rains of Bangladesh weakened its walls. The earthquake, which took place in the year of 1897 with the intensity of 8.5 on the Richter scale, shook the north part of Bangladesh along with Assam, and dealt a severe blow to the monastery. Subsequently, when the population around the *mahavihara* increased, the whole complex fell to a prey to brick vandals. They robbed the monastery of its bricks and terracotta bas-reliefs to use them to build their dwelling houses and roads.

The monastery remained hidden under the debris for a long time, and was brought to light again, in the year of 1807, by an English man, Dr. Buchanan Hamilton.

In the year of 1919, the government declared the monastery, under the Ancient Monument Preservation Act, to be a protected monument. A few years later, in the year of 1923, archeological excavation at the site of the monastery was taken at hand. The excavation carried out in 1925-26, led by archaeologist Rakhal Chandra Banarji exposed a great part of the *stupa*.

The excavation at the site was completed in the year of 1934. The successful excavation exposed up the whole of the monastery and the history of its construction.

The most of the finds at the monastery have been carried away from Bangladesh in the wake of the completion of the excavation. Some of the left-out finds are now at display in the national museum in Dhaka; and some others, in the museum adjacent to the monastery.

Though the monastery was built by Emperor Dharmapala, it was renovated, by some of his successors, in the *stupa* as well as in the monastic cells. A number of ornamental pedestals seem to have been installed in some cells during the renovations. 92 cells have the ornamental pedestal to hold a statue or an urn.

A brief description of the monastery

The huge Paharpur Monastery, built of fire-burnt bricks, laid in mud mortar, is a result of a single construction phase. It is almost quadrangular in shape, measuring 281.03 meters from north to south, and 280.11 meters from east to west. The monastery has 177 cells on the ground floor. All the cells are connected by a specious veranda, which is 2.4-2.7 meters in width and runs continuously all around. A flight of steps has gone down from the verandah to the inner courtyard in the middle of each wing. The basement wall of the verandah was decorated with a single row of terracotta plaques; a few of them can be seen now.

The main entrance of the monastery is on the north side in the middle. There are two pillared entrance halls, outer and inner, at the gateway. Besides the main entrance, there are two more narrow entrances to the monastery — one in the middle of its north-east corner and the other one in the middle of its east wing.

On the inner courtyard of the monastery, there are votive *stupas*, minor chapels, multitude of other structures such as kitchen, refectory and a huge *stupa* temple in the center. Except of the central *stupa*, the upper floors of the monastery are no more there.

The approximately 4.88 meters thick outer wall of the monastic cells works as the enclosure wall of the monastery. In its present ruinous state, the enclosure wall is 3.66-4.57 meters in height from the ground. Each of the cells, excluding the cells of the central block, measures approximately 4.27 meters by 4.11 meters. Out of 177 cells, 92 cells contain ornamental pedestals in the center. There are 45 cells on the north side and 44 cells in each side of the three other sides of the monastery.

There is a row of toilets, built on a platform, at the south-west corner of the monastery. The platform is connected with the south wing of the monastery by a 27 meters long raised gangway.

To build the Paharpur Monastery, the architectural design of the Salban Monastery at Mainamoti in Comilla — a district in the south-east part of Bangladesh — was followed. The unique Salban architectural design is the first in the world of its kind. In this type of design of a Buddhist monastery, the quadrangular shaped monastery has a central *stupa* on its inner compound surrounded by monastic cells laid out in a row. The Nalanda type Buddhist monastery is also of quadrangular shape, but without a temple/*stupa* on its inner compound. In the Nalanda type of Buddhist monastery, a temple is built on the outer compound to be used by one or more monasteries.

The brick foundation of the Paharpur Monastery has gone as deep as 12.19 meters under the ground, gradually getting broader with the increase of the depth. The height of the plinth of the Monastery is 3.66 meters above the ground; the thickness of the outer wall of the cell is 4.88 meters; and the foundation of the monastery has gone so deep as 12.19 meters — from all these facts we can deduce that the Monastery was a multistoried building. May be it was a three, four or five-storied building or it might have more stories than that.

A few more old structures, Gandheswari Temple, Bathing *ghat* (place), Satyapir Bhita — a *Tara* temple, can be seen in the outskirt of the Paharpur Monastery.

The whole Paharpur Monastery complex covers 11 hectares of land. And the monastery covers roughly 7.87 hectares of land.

Bibliography

Nazimuddin, A.	Paharpur, Department of Archaeology, 1975
Qadir, M.A.A.	A guide to Paharpur, Department of Archaeology, 1963
Nazimuddin, A	Mahasthan, Mainamati, Paharpur (in Bengali), Department of Archaeology, 1997 (3rd Edition)
Dikshit, K.N.	Excavation at Paharpur, 1938
Dikshit, K.N.	Memoirs of the Archaeological Survey of India, 1955
Chakrabarti, D.K.	Ancient Bangladesh, The University Press Limited, 2001
Hossain, M.M; Alam, M.S.	Paharpur - The World Cultural Heritage, Department of Archaeology, 2004
Majumdar, R.C.	History of Bengal, Vol. 1 (2nd Impression), Dhaka University, 1964
Mitra, S.C.	Jessore-Khulnar Itihas (in Bengali), Rupantar, 2001 (3rd Edition, reprint)
Musa, M.A.	Journal of Bengal Art, Vol. 4, 1999
Gail A.J.,	Journal of Bengal Art, Vol. 4, 1999

www.ingramcontent.com/pod-product-compliance
Lightning Source LLC
Chambersburg PA
CBHW042324150426
43192CB00001B/42